THERE'S A ZOO IN MY POO

First published 2020 in Macmillan by Pan Macmillan Australia Pty Ltd
1 Market Street, Sydney, New South Wales, Australia, 2000

Cataloguing-in-Publication entry is available
from the National Library of Australia
http://catalogue.nla.gov.au

Internal design by Billy Blue Creative
Typeset in 12/16.5pt Carniola SemiBold
Printed in China by Hang Tai Printing Co. Limited

10 9 8 7 6 5 4

THERE'S A ZOO IN MY POO

by Professor
Felice Jacka

illustrated by
Rob Craw

MACMILLAN
Pan Macmillan Australia

Contents

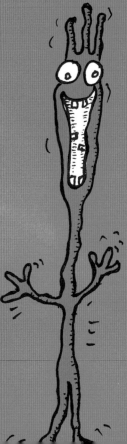

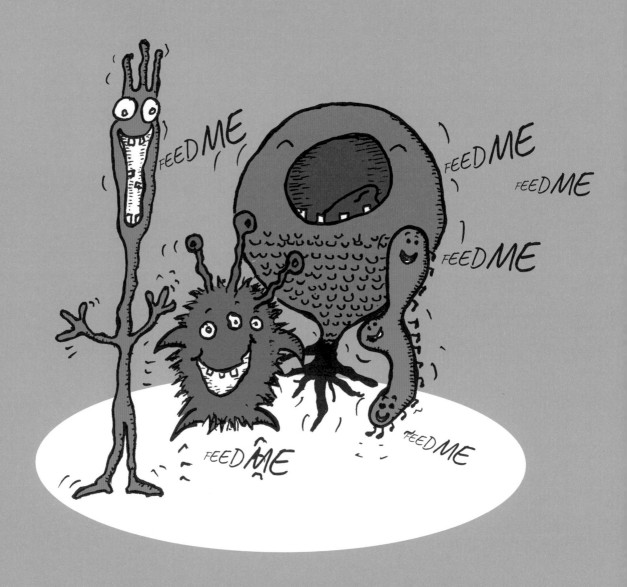

Did you know
there's a Zoo in your Poo?
It needs a Zookeeper
and that Keeper is YOU!

That Zoo is created by
all kinds of creatures
that live on us and in us,
with all kinds of features.

They can't live without
us and us without them.
These microscopic bugs
on which we depend.

7

YOU ARE A BUG!

Trillions of tiny bugs live in and on you, me and everyone.

These tiny bugs are called microbiota, and they are too small to see without a microscope.

They are made up of things like viruses, fungi (like yeast), and organisms called archaea. But most of our microbiota are bacteria – and there are lots of them.

About . . .

40,000,000,000,000
(that's trillions!)

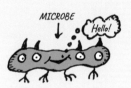

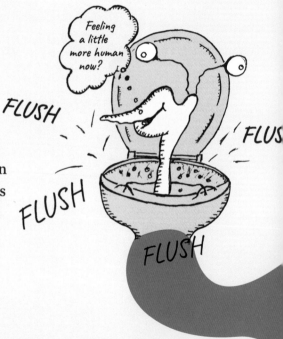

This is about the same number of cells you have in your body. Because of the BIG number of bugs within you, you are as much bug as you are human. These bugs in your guts make up a big part of your poo so once that poo is out of you, you actually become slightly more human than bug . . . **for a while!**

You might think that's creepy
or just straight out weird.
But this world, it is wonderful
and not to be feared.

These creatures are warriors
they battle in your guts.
Trillions of tiny fighters
turning bad bugs into DUST.

Battle of the bugs

We can't live without these bugs and they can't live without us.

We give them a lovely home and they help to keep us healthy and strong. But only if we look after them properly. If we don't look after them properly, some of these bugs . . .

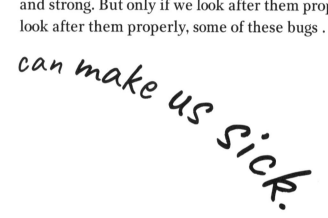

can make us sick.

But how do they do this?
How can they be kept strong?
This is where you come in,
Zookeeper, to help these bugs along.

This story of you
and your microscopic stew
begins in your gob
and ends up as a Poo!

Follow the food to see how
your body turns it into fuel.

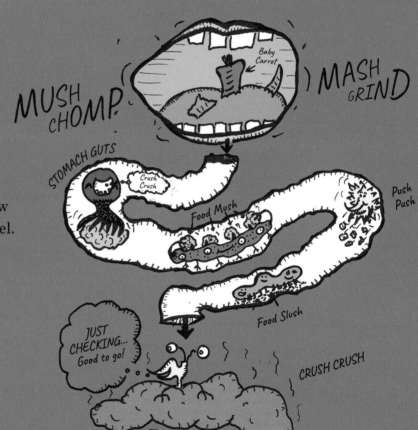

MUSH
CHOMP

MASH
GRIND

Baby
Carrot

STOMACH GUTS

Crush
Crush

Food Mush

Push
Push

Food Slush

JUST
CHECKING...
Good to go!

CRUSH CRUSH

From your mouth to your bum

The largest number of bugs live in your digestive tract.

This includes your mouth, your oesophagus (the pipe that links your mouth to your stomach), your stomach, and your small and large intestines. These bugs do many jobs, but the most important one is breaking down certain parts of foods for you.

Your body is very busy, doing complicated things every second of every day.

It needs fuel to make all its cells work, to grow bones and muscles, to help your brain to think and learn and remember things, to fight illnesses and infections and repair injuries. It gets this fuel from food.

What was the last big meal you ate? Maybe it was something yummy like a tuna and salad sandwich made with multigrain bread.

ALL ABOARD THE POO TRAIN

FIRST STOP

Mouth and stomach

Once you bite your sandwich and start to chew, saliva mixes in with the chewed-up food. Saliva has mucus in it, and this is the slimy stuff that helps the food to travel down your oesophagus.

Once the food is in your tummy, powerful enzymes and acids break it down into lots of little bits so it can be absorbed into your blood to be fuel for your body. A lot of this happens in the small intestine.

I knew that!

The oesophagus is the pipe that squeezes in and out to push chewed-up food down into your tummy...

The small intestine

not so small, after all

The small intestine is actually about 6 metres long. With all its nooks, crannies and projections (called **villi**), it is about the size of **10 table tennis tables.**

THE
SMALL INTESTINE
CHAMPIONSHIP

BILOPHILA WADSWORTHIA **VS** LACTOBACILLUS

THE VILLI GRANDSTAND

A lot of digestive action takes place in the small intestine. More enzymes are released, and something called bile helps to break down fats.

The villi that line parts of the small intestine look like tiny fingers. They wave about and absorb a lot of the broken-down, mushed-up food so that it can get into your blood.

But that's not all that happens in the small intestine. There are also plenty of bacteria and other microorganisms down here.

Bug vs bug

Some of the bugs – like *Bilophila Wadsworthia* – love the kind of fats found in foods like fatty meats, bacon and sausages. These fats encourage the liver and gall bladder to release bile, and *Bilophila* like bile.

But *Bilophila* bugs may make us sick. People with a range of nasty diseases have more *Bilophila Wadsworthia* and that's why we think they aren't friendly bugs.

But we also have good bugs in our small intestine, such as the various *Lactobacillus* species that are found in yoghurt and cheeses as well as other fermented foods. We want these bugs around because they help our immune system, our guts, and might even help with allergies and eczema.

16

The LARGE intestine

This is where the **really heavy bug** action takes place.
It's much shorter than the small intestine, but it's called 'large'
because it's much thicker.

There are up to 1000 different species of bacteria here in your
personal Zoo – the greatest number of microbiota in your body.
In fact, the weight of all the bugs that live in your large intestine
is about **the same weight as your brain!**

These bugs are in charge of breaking down all the different
bits of food that your enzymes can't break down. This
is a very important job. But as well as this, the bugs in your
large intestine do many more important things that help to keep
you strong and healthy.

BUGS IN OUR GUTS

People with lots of different types of gut bugs seem to be healthier than those who don't have a variety of bugs. This may be because the more different types of bugs you have, the less likely one particular group of bugs will 'take over' your guts and make you sick.

Having lots of different sorts of bugs in our guts also means that we are better able to manage if we suddenly have to battle a bad bug.

The power of bugs

Another of the important things our gut bugs do is to help us digest new foods. If we have a sudden change in diet or start to eat something new, we need certain types of bugs to help us digest these new foods. Having a big range of gut bugs means we can adapt to different types of foods quickly. Japanese people, for example, have special bacteria in their guts that can break down seaweed.

Gut bugs also help us deal with nasty substances in the environment. We're only just learning about this, but it looks like our gut bugs may also deal with potentially dangerous chemicals, such as pesticides and other types of pollution.

SUPER BUGS to the RESCUE

To be a good Keeper
and have a happy Zoo,
you need a wide range of bugs
to live inside of you.

BAD BUGS
KEEP OUT

As busy as a bug

Your gut bugs have many jobs. They get energy from foods that could not be broken down further up in the stomach and small intestine by your own enzymes. In particular, they deal with the important dietary **fibre**, which comes from plant foods.

FIBRE IS GOOD!

100% Great! Yum!

VERY IMPORTANT molecule
↓

When the final bits of your sandwich get to your large intestine, the bacteria that live there take the bits that can't be digested by your enzymes and break it down by fermenting it.

This fermentation process is similar to what happens when cheese and yoghurt are made. It produces many important molecules such as short chain fatty acids. These short chain fatty acids are small parcels that act as messages to talk to your brain and influence the way your genes work to make proteins. We are learning more and more about the many different actions of the molecules that are created by our gut bugs. Short chain fatty acids are also fuel for the cells in our intestines and are very important in keeping our gut healthy.

The large intestine bugs are possibly the busiest bugs in your body.

Nerve 1 to Nerve 2:

Yep!

Are you receiving me?

They create different types of vitamins and things called neurotransmitters – chemical messengers that allow nerves to talk to each other.

They also play a big role in running our immune systems; our immune system fights infections, heals wounds and helps us to stay well. They also affect our body weight and blood sugar levels, and even the health of our brains!

Once all the bugs have broken down those last bits of food and turned them into fuel and fermentation molecules, then any left-over bits of food, along with lots and lots of bacteria, leave your body in the form of a poo.

Now we're getting to the good stuff!

YOUR POO
AND YOU

It has been said, 'You are what you eat!'
What goes in must come out with some squeezing.
Your poo is a clue to the health of this stew
and your gut bugs need a good feeding.

Your poo can tell you a lot about your health.

In many countries, toilets are designed so you can have a good look at your poo before you flush it away.

OK. What am I looking at? GIVE ME A CLUE...

What a fine specimen

Bristol Stool Chart

The Bristol Stool Chart helps you tell if your poo is a good, healthy poo – or not.

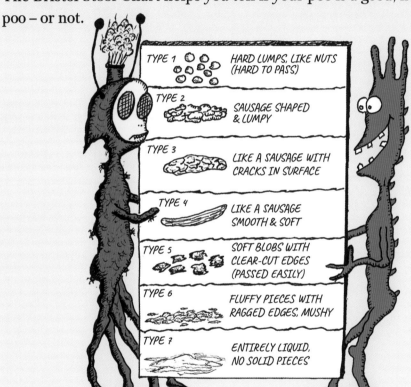

TYPE 1 — HARD LUMPS, LIKE NUTS (HARD TO PASS)

TYPE 2 — SAUSAGE SHAPED & LUMPY

TYPE 3 — LIKE A SAUSAGE WITH CRACKS IN SURFACE

TYPE 4 — LIKE A SAUSAGE SMOOTH & SOFT

TYPE 5 — SOFT BLOBS WITH CLEAR-CUT EDGES (PASSED EASILY)

TYPE 6 — FLUFFY PIECES WITH RAGGED EDGES, MUSHY

TYPE 7 — ENTIRELY LIQUID, NO SOLID PIECES

Poo 3, 4 or 5 are the best kinds of poo. But if most of your poos are not a 3, 4 or 5, then you might need to think about what you're feeding your Zoo and ask yourself:

Am I being the best Zookeeper I can be?

MUCUS! NOT SNOTS, BOOGERS OR LOOGIES

There is much to know
'bout the insides of your tummy.
And it's to do with some stuff
that is gooey and runny.

Up your nose there is mucus
and some call it 'snot'.
But does it line your guts?
Oh, yes. I kid you not!

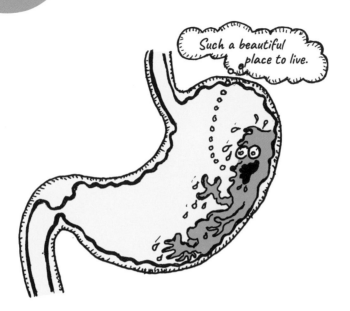

Mucus is in your nose (snot) but it's also in your guts.

Your large intestine is covered with a lining of mucus that helps to keep you healthy. If something affects this mucus lining – for example, if you don't eat enough plant foods with fibre in them – then the lining of your guts can become less healthy and strong. This means that the stuff that should stay in your guts, like bits of food and bugs themselves, could sneak through and get into your blood.

25

Sneaky bug ALERT

When this happens, your immune system senses these intruders, goes on **HIGH ALERT**, and reacts with something called 'inflammation'. This low-level inflammation may increase your chances of developing all sorts of diseases. In fact, inflammation is so important to understanding our health that we need to talk about it a bit more.

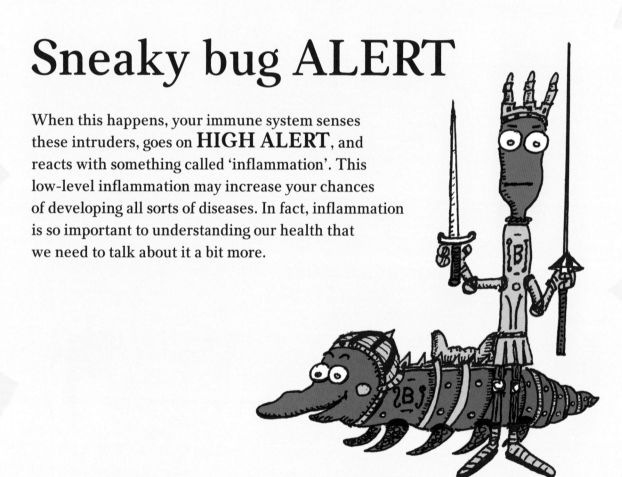

Armour for your insides

Your immune system is your body's very own superhero.
You wouldn't survive long without it. When you get sick from an
infection such as a virus, your immune system springs into action
to battle the infection and make you well. If you cut yourself while
you're helping to chop vegetables – or break your arm playing
football – your immune system saves the day and heals the injury.

But it does a lot more than that:

✓ *Your immune system attacks and kills cancer cells
when they appear.*

✓ *It protects you from many diseases.*

✓ *It affects the health of your brain.*

In fact, your immune system is central
to pretty much everything your body
does. That's why it's so important
to keep it strong.

Your gut bugs play a very
important role in operating your
immune system and keeping
inflammation away so you need
to keep your bugs happy.

Brain drain

Who would have thought it?
Who would have thunk it?
Keep your Zoo happy
and your brain
it just loves it.

Your gut and your brain talk to each other all the time via something called the vagus nerve. Most of the signals go from your gut to your brain and many of the molecules produced by the gut bacteria, such as short chain fatty acids and neurotransmitters, are used as part of this messaging system.

Scientists believe that the microbes that live on and in us are important to the health of our brains, including reducing inflammation in our brains and improving what we call 'brain plasticity'.

The 'plastic' aspect of your brain (the ability of a part of the brain called the hippocampus to shrink and grow) is very important for you to be able to learn and remember things. If you can't learn and remember, you will struggle with school, work and . . . everything!

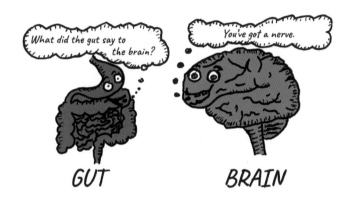

Poo transplants

The bugs that live in your gut may affect your behaviour. One of the strongest clues that this is true comes from experiments with poo transplants. For example, when scientists swapped poo between mice that were normally very anxious and mice that were more relaxed, the nervous mice became calm and the calm mice became nervous!

BABY BUG

*From the day we are born
we create our own Zoo.
The dirt that you play in
can help with this too.*

We don't think there are many bugs in the womb in which you grew, if any. But babies are exposed to bacteria during and soon after birth. As a very young baby, you had different gut bugs from your parents. But they started to look more like theirs by the time you were about three.

Everyone's bugs are a bit different – almost like everyone has unique fingerprints. Breastmilk from mothers contains important bacteria called *Bifidobacteria*, but also food for the *Bifidobacteria* to eat so that they can grow and make more bugs. In fact, there is food in breastmilk that ONLY bacteria can eat.

Mice bred without bacteria (germ-free mice) have very different brains from normal mice born with bacteria. The bacteria an animal is exposed to and that sets up home in the gut at the very start of its life influences the way its brain grows. We think this is also true for us.

But the other important thing that happens in early life is the development of the immune system. Our gut bacteria play a big role in this in the first days, weeks and months of our life.

We know that the bugs that move into our guts when we are born are very important to the way our bodies and brains grow. *Bifidobacteria* seem to be particularly important in training our baby immune systems. So what, apart from breastmilk, are the things that affect the way our personal Zoo is formed?

Dog licks and mud pies

Do your parents or your teachers tell you to stop playing in the dirt?
Well, maybe they shouldn't quite as much.

We need to be exposed to bugs in the dirt, as well as in our wider
world (such as in the forests and the oceans), to keep our Zoos
diverse and healthy.

Babies crawl around the ground and put EVERYTHING in their mouths. Even really disgusting things.

Now we think this might be very important for their developing immune systems. When we are babies, our gut bacteria train our immune system. The more different types of bacteria we are exposed to, the more our immune systems are able to grow and get strong.

Another way you can meet lots of bugs is by contact with animals. Children who grow up with pets in the house, or on farms with lots of animals, are less likely to have allergies and we think this is because of their stronger (trained) immune systems. Brothers and sisters can also help your immune system as they bring more bacteria into the home for your own bugs to learn from.

Your brother is a germ.

Best bugs

Some species of *Bifidobacteria* and *Lactobacillus* are types of bugs called 'probiotics' – this means that they've proven themselves to be good for our health.

There are some special *Bifidobacteria* that help to train your immune system when you are a baby. As you grow up, many types of *Bifidobacteria* do important things, including protecting the lining of your gut and making something called 'butyrate', which is a short chain fatty acid that reduces inflammation and has other benefits for brains.

Some types of *Bifidobacteria*, along with *Lactobacillus* and *Propionibacteria* can even make B-group vitamins to keep us healthy. Particular species of *Bifidobacteria* and *Lactobacillus* also make neurotransmitters, including one called 'GABA' that can make us feel less anxious.

We want these BUGS AROUND!

Animals, dirt and brothers and sisters are all important for having strong and diverse gut bugs, but the most important thing affecting the diversity and health of your Zoo is **what you eat.**

FEED YOUR ZOO

Veggies are great, with fruit,
seeds and nuts.
Add grains and some legumes
to make happy guts.

Plant foods are wonderful,
all kinds will do.
The more types the better
for the Zoo in your Poo.

We want to keep our gut bugs healthy and happy. And the most important thing you do every single day is to eat.

What foods do your bugs need to grow and thrive and keep you healthy? And what DON'T they like?

BROCCOLI

POTATO

WHOLEGRAIN BREAD

SPINACH

FISH

APPLE

BERRIES

CARROT

BANANA

ZUCCHINI

ALMONDS

ONION

PORRIDGE

STRAWBERRY

BROWN RICE

WALNUTS

CASHEWS

MANDARIN

Plants rule

Bugs eat fibre so that is the most important part of your diet when it comes to feeding your Zoo!

The bacteria in your guts ferment fibre to make the molecules that affect all the parts of your body and brain. *Bifidobacteria*, a really good bug, thrives on fibre and uses it to produce the short chain fatty acid butyrate. Without fibre, our bugs can't do what they're supposed to do.

But many of us don't eat nearly enough fibre. This might be a **BIG** problem for our Zoo. We may even be starving some of our important bugs out of existence.

MMM, PLANT FOOD ABOUT TIME, I'M STARVING

TOMATO

CARROT

CELERY

EGGPLANT

Plant foods also have something in them called 'polyphenols'. Polyphenols are another part of plant foods that our own enzymes can't break down, so we need our gut bugs to do it for us. These polyphenols are very good for our guts and our health and they help to give plant foods their different colours. Polyphenols might even help us avoid putting on too much weight!

Plant foods have many other important things in them that are good for our bodies and brains.

Nature is very clever and provides what we need to thrive.

Vegetables and fruit give bad bugs the boot

We need to eat lots of different types of vegetables and fruit every day to feed our gut bugs. There's lots of fibre in the skins so eat these too.

If you eat a rainbow of fruit and vegetables: red, green and yellow capsicums; oranges; red and green apples; carrots; broccoli and spinach; tomatoes; onions; mushrooms; bananas; pears and purple berries (Top Tip: frozen fruit and vegetables are fine as well!), all these different colours will feed your bugs and keep them healthy and happy.

People who eat 30 different types of plant foods every week (fruits, vegetables, wholegrains, nuts and seeds and legumes) have more different types of bugs in their guts than those who eat fewer than ten.

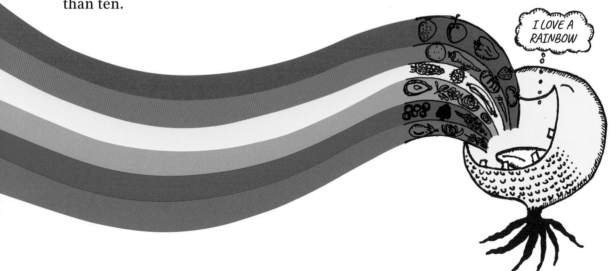

I LOVE A RAINBOW

Grains! Great for bodies and brains

Grains, and particularly 'wholegrains', are excellent for your bugs. While many grains are processed and not so good for you (white bread and cakes: we're talking about YOU!), the grains that are not processed contain lots of nutrients and fibre.

Porridge; wholegrain breakfast cereal; brown pasta; wholegrain (particularly sourdough) breads; rye bread; pumpernickel bread; couscous; quinoa; barley; brown, red, purple and black rice; and pasta made from legumes, all provide lots of different types of fibre for your bugs to ferment.

Wholegrains also have something called 'beta-glucans' in them, which are very helpful to your immune system and reduce inflammation. In fact, wholegrains are one of the top food groups for your body.

TOP TIPS

✗ Eat porridge with some yoghurt and frozen berries for breakfast.
✗ Or sourdough rye toast with sardines or avocado or even peanut butter.
✗ Add barley to your soups, and cold rice or quinoa to your salads.

41

Bean there

Beans make you fart
but that's quite okay.
It's a sign that
your good bugs are
working away.

42

Legumes are things like chickpeas, lentils, baked beans, black beans, pinto beans, red beans, adzuki beans, cannellini beans, kidney beans, lima beans (all beans really), and green peas. These have **lots** and lots of fibre, so feed your Zoo with beans, beans, beans.

Beans can sometimes make you fart, but **bean farts are good**. They're the sound of your bugs at work, breaking down and fermenting all that wonderful fibre. And if you're not used to eating beans, you might fart even more. But your gut will adapt, and your Zoo will be grateful to you.

TOP TIP:

Add a tin of lentils or chickpeas to your spaghetti bolognaise for dinner. You'll be looking after your Zoo, as well as feeding you.

CHICKPEAS

Tickle, tickle, good bug!

Fat facts

Fats are yummy and make us feel full. They also help your body run all its systems. But some types of fats feed the bad bugs, and others feed the good bugs.

When you eat avocados, oily fish (like sardines and salmon) and olive oil – the fats in these foods make your bugs and guts happy. *Bifidobacteria* are good guys and they really **LOVE** the sorts of fats that are found in fish, nuts and olive oil.

But fatty and processed meats, like sausages and bacon, have fats that can cause inflammation. They also feed bugs like *Bilophila wadsworthia* (see page 16).

A little bit of butter is okay, but not too much.

TOP TIPS

✗ Eat avocado and sardines on wholegrain toast for breakfast.
✗ Add avocado, salmon or tuna and olive oil to a big salad.
✗ You'll be doing yourself and your Zoo a big favour.

AVOCADOS FOR EYES AND A TASTE FOR FISH

And if it helps your Zoo, then it also helps you.

um. Yum. Yum. Yum. Yum. Yum. Yum. Yum.

On nuts and seeds, good bugs will feed

Nuts and seeds are nature's perfect little food bombs: they have lots of fibre, lots of healthy fats, and lots of protein, vitamins and minerals for your body and brain to soak up and use.

There are so many nuts and seeds you can eat. There are cashews, almonds, brazil nuts, chestnuts, walnuts, hazelnuts, macadamia nuts, pumpkin seeds, sesame seeds, and sunflower seeds. All of these have different sorts of benefits for you and they're all delicious.

Eat nuts that haven't had salt added to them – this is important as salt can hurt good bugs such as *Lactobacillus* (see page 16). Also, keep your nuts and seeds in the fridge so they stay fresh. When the oils in nuts and seeds go 'off,' they're not as good for you and they don't taste as nice.

Try to eat a wide range of these nuts and seeds. They make a really great snack for you and your Zoo and will keep you feeling full.

Yum. Yum. Yum. Yum. Yum. Yum. Yum. Y

Starch is cool

Another important part of your food is called 'resistant starch'. This happens when we cook potato, pasta or rice and then let it cool down. Even when we heat this type of food up again, the resistant starch remains. Bugs really like to eat resistant starch and they use it to ferment and create all those important things like short chain fatty acids.

There's also natural resistant starch in bananas that are not too ripe, as well as in many wholegrains, like oats, pearl barley, rice and rye bread, and in legumes.

As if you needed another good reason to get wholegrains and legumes into your diet!

Fermented food for an awesome mood

Yoghurt, cheese, Japanese foods such as miso soup, fermented vegetables such as kimchi from Korea, or sauerkraut from Europe, and drinks like kefir (fermented water or milk) and kombucha (fermented tea) are all fermented foods.

Fermented foods have bacteria that have been added or occur naturally. These bacteria actually do some of the work of fermenting (breaking down) the foods before they even get into your mouth.

FERMENTATION

Before we had fridges, fermentation was used to stop foods from going bad. There are examples of fermented foods in countries all over the world. And we think that these foods are good for us. But why?

When the bugs ferment foods, they create all sorts of molecules like short and long chain fatty acids, neurotransmitters, and something called 'biogenics'. And we're starting to find out all the many important things that these molecules do in our body and brains. Eating or drinking fermented foods is a quick way to get these molecules into our bodies.

Some fermented foods also contain 'prebiotics', which is the food that bugs ferment to create these important molecules – and some can even contain probiotic bugs themselves, such as *Lactobacillus*.

So, eat or drink fermented foods. They can add new bugs to your guts (remember, scientists think that diversity is good) and give them food to eat.

WHAT NOT
TO EAT

If every day, junk food comes your way,
and that's what goes into your tummy,
bad bugs will thrive, good bugs will die,
and your poo will be too hard or runny.

If you want to be the BEST Zookeeper you can be, there are some foods that you need to avoid.

Greedy guts

Our brains love junk foods with lots of fat and sugar and salt in them. These foods might make us feel happy for a short time but they are REALLY not good for us in the long term.

People didn't eat much junk food in the old days. They were a special weekend treat. But, now, these foods are everywhere we look – at the snack bar at the swimming pool, at school or the supermarket, or when we walk down the street. On average, young people eat seven of these sorts of foods every day.

THE JUNK-FOOD LIST IS LONG:

chips (hot chips and crisps), sausage rolls, fried dim sims, potato cakes, fried chicken, fatty hamburgers, bacon and sausages, macaroni and cheese, soft (fizzy) drinks, cordials, energy drinks, doughnuts, cakes, ice creams, lollies and chocolate, sweetened 'breakfast' or snack bars, breakfast cereals with lots of added sugars, thickshakes, white bread, chocolate sandwich spreads, highly processed cheeses . . .

Junk foods are really bad for your bugs because they have:

ADDED FATS.
Junk foods are often made with types of fats that increase inflammation and feed the bad bugs, like *Bilophila Wadsworthia*. (Remember bile, page 16?)

SUGARS.
We know that foods with added sugars, like lollies, doughnuts, biscuits and soft drinks, can harm our immune system, and affect our brain plasticity, body weight and health. But recent research in animals also suggests that when there is too much sugar in the blood, it damages the lining of the gut.

And artificial sugars may not be any better. When scientists feed mice artificial sugars (like the sugar in diet soft drinks), these seem to help unhealthy bacteria grow and also affect metabolism in a way that can increase body weight. So even though they don't have any energy themselves, these pretend sugars might affect your body in a way that is the same as if they *did* have lots of energy.

'EMULSIFIERS':

These are things that are added to almost all processed foods (ice creams often have lots of them) to help the fats and the liquids in the foods to mix together. But scientific experiments suggest that they might also strip away the mucus lining on your gut (see page 25). This lining helps to keep everything in your gut and not let it escape into your blood and cause inflammation.

UGH! I've been emulsified!

SALT.

Junk foods often have lots of salt added to them, and this can increase inflammation and hurt our good *Lactobacillus* bugs.

Brain power

Who would have thought it?
Who would have thunk it?
The junk food I ate,
my brain, it just shrunk it!

Junk foods also seem to have a direct and nasty effect on brains. They affect a part of the brain called the hippocampus (remember me, page 29?). This is the part that helps you to learn and remember things. You need it all through your life, for studying, working and having a happy life. And we now know that people who eat lots of junk food have a smaller hippocampus.

PEANUT-SIZE
BRAIN

So, there are many, many, reasons why you should eat these sorts of foods as a once-a-week treat, not as an everyday part of your diet.

Finally, it's important to give your bugs an occasional break. Eating all the time can make it harder for your gut bugs to do their jobs. Try to have gaps between your meals and snacks so that your Zoo gets some time out (everybody needs a rest sometimes!)

So be a good Keeper
to the Zoo in your Poo.
Look after your body
and it will look after you.

RECIPES
FOR YOUR
ZOO

Here are a few easy and fun ideas that you can try yourself. You might need some help from a grown-up at the start, but pretty soon you'll be able to chop and cook food by yourself.

Zoo-Poo Stew

YOU'LL NEED

> legumes
> onion or leek
> garlic
> sweet potato
> potato
> pumpkin
> zucchini

> mushrooms
> leaves like spinach
> or chard
> rice or barley
> Use brown rice or
> black rice or even
> wild rice.

Barley gives a lovely
chewy texture.
> tinned tomatoes and
> tomato paste
> stock cubes (beef,
> chicken or vegetable)
> extra virgin olive oil

Do you have a slow-cooker (crockpot) at home? Or a big pot to go on the stove? You'll need one of these.

WHAT TO DO

1. Chop up the onions or leek, and the garlic
2. Chop up the vegetables (except leaves) into cubes big enough to eat easily
3. Add the onion/leek and garlic, the vegetables, a tin of tomatoes, a big tablespoon of tomato paste, and stock cubes to a big pot of water. You can adjust all of these depending on how much you want to make.
4. Add the lentils/beans and the rice or barley (make sure the water covers everything)
5. Cook your Zoo-Poo Stew on a low heat until everything is soft (put in the leaves at the end)

You can add a lamb hock or similar if you want to add some meat to the stew. You can also add in fresh or dried herbs if you have them – the more plant foods the better!

Farty Toast

This is pretty easy.
Toast some wholegrain bread (remember, your gut bugs love wholegrains) then add some tinned baked beans on top (the low-salt variety). That's it!

TOP TIP

* ⚹ You could also put extra virgin olive oil on the toast because this has LOTS of polyphenols.

Fermenting For Fun

Making your own fermented milk (kefir) or tea (kombucha) or vegetables at home is really easy, cheap and fun. You'll just need some big jars. You can get the 'scoby' (which is the bacteria that do the fermenting) from a health food shop along with the simple instructions. You don't need a scoby for fermented vegetables – just a big glass jar and some veggies!

Better-Bog-Burgers

YOU'LL NEED

- a food processor
- 2 tins of lentils (or pre-cooked ones)
- 1 onion and 2 garlic cloves
- 1 cup of walnuts and sunflower seeds (you can use different nuts and seeds if you like)
- 1–2 carrots (you can grate these if you like)
- 2 eggs
- 2 tablespoons of tomato paste
- half a cup of wholemeal flour
- some breadcrumbs
- some extra virgin olive oil

WHAT TO DO

Blend the lentils, onions, garlic, nuts and seeds, and carrot together in the food processor, then mix in two eggs, the tomato paste and the flour until it starts to stick together. If you like, you can add some fresh herbs, or dried ones like oregano.

Form the goo into lots of patties with your hands, then roll in the breadcrumbs and fry in a pan with the olive oil. VOILA!

TOP TIP

✗ You can eat these in a bun with lettuce, tomato and cheese, just like a hamburger. Don't forget the tomato or BBQ sauce! You'll soon be pooing like a champion.

Bug Breakfasts

Chia pudding

Fill a jar a third of the way up with chia seeds (you can get these from the supermarket), and then fill the jar up with milk, coconut milk or water, or any other type of milk you like. Add some vanilla to make it extra yummy.

Put the lid of the jar on and give it a good shake and put it on the bench where you'll see it. Then continue to give it a good shake every time you walk past the bench until the chia seeds start to expand and you're sure they're not going to clump up down at the bottom of the jar. This only takes three or four shakes. Then put the jar in the fridge overnight.

TOP TIP

- ✗ You can eat your chia pudding with grated coconut, frozen berries, apples and bananas, or any other sort of fruit you like. You can also add nuts and honey for extra yumminess!

Bircher muesli

Get some yummy untoasted muesli, preferably with dried fruit and nuts (you can even make this yourself), grate some apple into it, cover it with milk and put it in the fridge overnight. You can add some honey (bugs like honey) to make it sweet and even put some frozen berries on top!

Bye, for real this time!